Explore!

VICTORIANS

Jane Bingham

WAYLAND

First published in 2014 by Wayland

Copyright © Wayland 2014

Wayland
338 Euston Road
London NW1 3BH

Wayland Australia
Level 17/207 Kent Street
Sydney, NSW 2000

Produced for Wayland by
White-Thomson Publishing
www.wtpub.co.uk
+44 (0)843 208 7460

Editor: Jane Bingham
Designer: Tim Mayer
Picture researcher: Jane Bingham
Illustrations for step-by-step: Peter Bull
Proof reader: Lucy Ross

A cataloguing record for this title is available
from the British Library.

ISBN 978 0 7502 8037 2

Dewey Number 941'.081-dc23

10 9 8 7 6 5 4 3 2 1

Printed in Malaysia

Wayland is a division of Hachette Children's
Books, an Hachette UK company

www.hachette.co.uk

Picture acknowledgements:
The author and publisher would like to thank the
following agencies and people for allowing these
pictures to be reproduced:

Cover (top left) The Fleming-Wyfold Art
Foundation /The Bridgeman Art Library; (top
right) stable/Shutterstock; (bottom left) Jon
Le-Bon/Shutterstock; (bottom right) stephen/
Shutterstock; p.1 (left) Victorian Traditions/
Shutterstock; (right) stephen/Shutterstock; p.3
Stocksnapper/ Shutterstock; p.4 Wikimedia;
p.5 (top) stephen/Shutterstock; (bottom)
Nicku/ Dreamstime; p.6 Wikimedia; p.7 (top)
Antonio Abrignani/Shutterstock; (bottom)
Lucascao/Dreamstime; p.8 Wikimedia; p.9
(top) Malgorzata Kistryn/Shutterstock; (bottom)
Library of Congress; p.10 Victorian Traditions/
Shutterstock; p.11 (top) Antonio Abrignani/
Shutterstock; (bottom) Andrew Gritt/ Creative
Commons; p.12 jennyt/Shutterstock; p.13
(top) Private Collection/The Bridgeman Art
Library; (bottom) chippix/Shutterstock; p.14
Whiskybottle/Dreamstime; p.15 (top) Unholy
Vault Designs/Shutterstock; (bottom) Wikimedia;
p.16 The Fleming-Wyfold Art Foundation /The
Bridgeman Art Library; p.17 (top) Joegough/
Dreamstime; (bottom) Stockcreations/
Dreamstime; p.18 Allison Achauer/Shutterstock;
p.19 (top) Subhra2jyoti/ Dreamstime; (bottom)
Wikimedia; p.20 Pixel Memoirs/Shutterstock;
p.21(top) Angelina Dimitrova/Shutterstock;
(bottom) Wikimedia; p.22 Jitloac/Shutterstock;
p.23 (top) Stocksnapper/Shutterstock;
(bottom) Zambezishark /Dreamstime; p.24
Morphart Creation/Shutterstock; p.25 (top)
Sampete/ Dreamstime; (bottom) Wikimedia;
p.28 Wikimedia; p.29 (stamp) Doctor Jools/
Shutterstock; (bicycle) Stocksnapper/
Shutterstock; (Christmas card) Victorian
Traditions/Shutterstock; (light bulb) Allison
Achauer/Shutterstock.

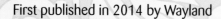

Contents

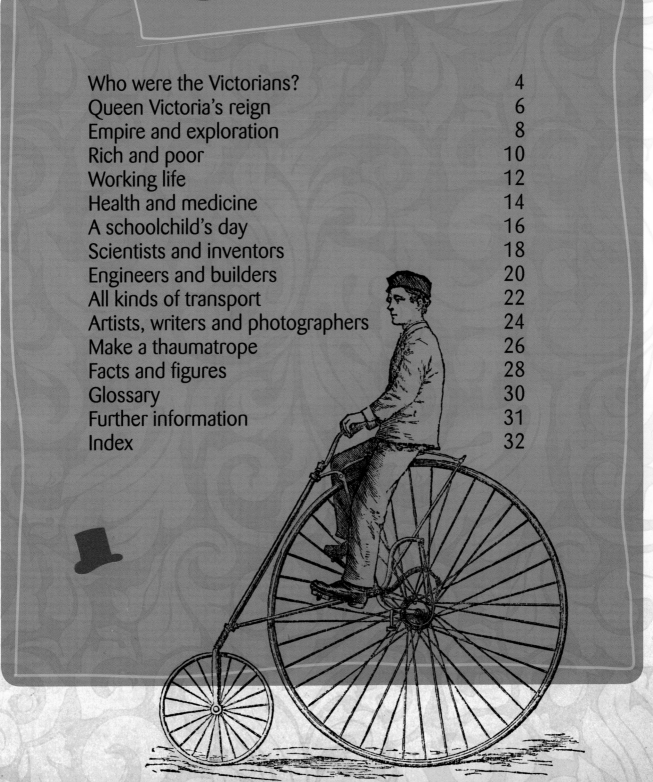

Who were the Victorians?

Queen Victoria ruled Britain and its empire from 1837 to 1901. This 64-year period is called the Victorian age. The people who lived in Britain in Victoria's reign are known as the Victorians. They lived through a time of great progress and change.

A changing nation

In the Victorian period, Britain became an industrial nation. Factories were built, towns grew rapidly, and a network of railways stretched across the country. Britain exported goods and machinery all over the world. Some Victorians grew extremely rich, but life was very hard for the working classes.

This portrait shows the 18-year-old Queen Victoria at the start of her long reign.

An enormous empire

Queen Victoria ruled over an enormous empire. The British Empire included Canada in the north and Australia and New Zealand in the south. It also covered most of India and parts of Africa. The British built schools, hospitals and churches all over their Empire, and the Victorian way of life spread around the world.

The Victorian period is often known as the age of steam. As well as building steam engines and steamships, the Victorians relied on steam power in their factories.

Remembering the Victorians

The Victorians helped to shape our modern world. Today, our towns and cities are filled with Victorian houses, churches and public buildings, and many railways built in the Victorian age are still in use. Electric lights, telephones and bicycles were all introduced during Victoria's reign. The Victorian period also produced some outstanding writers. The novels of Charles Dickens and Charlotte and Emily Brontë are still enjoyed today.

Charles Dickens wrote 15 novels. His stories bring the Victorian age to life.

Victoria's reign

Victoria was the daughter of a British prince and a German princess. Her father died when she was a baby and she was brought up by her mother and a governess. When she was just 18, her uncle, King William IV, died and she was crowned Queen of Great Britain and Ireland.

Victoria and Albert

At the age of 21, Victoria married her cousin, Albert of Saxe-Coburg and Gotha. The royal couple were devoted to each other and they had nine children. Prince Albert worked hard to encourage British trade, industry and science. He was a great support to his wife, but he died young, at the age of 42. Victoria never recovered from Albert's death. She dressed in black for the rest of her life.

This painting shows Victoria and Albert with five of their children. They loved to spend time together with their family.

British prime ministers

During Victoria's reign, Britain had two outstanding prime ministers. William Ewart Gladstone led the Whig party (also known as the Liberals). He wanted parliament to have more power and campaigned to increase the number of voters. Benjamin Disraeli led the Tory Party (also known as the Conservatives). He was a great supporter of the British Empire.

In 1876, Benjamin Disraeli persuaded Queen Victoria to take the title 'Empress of India'.

Last years

Queen Victoria reigned until her death at the age of 81. After she died, her eldest son was crowned King Edward VII. The Victorian age came to an end and the Edwardian period began.

People all over the British Empire erected statues of Queen Victoria. This statue is in Victoria Park, Hong Kong.

Empire and exploration

By the 1890s, the British Empire covered one fifth of all of the world's land. Some countries in the Empire, such as Canada, Australia and New Zealand, had been discovered by British explorers. Others were won in wars in Victoria's reign.

This map was made in 1886. It shows the countries of the British Empire coloured pink.

A growing Empire

In India, British and Indian troops fought a bitter war known as the Indian Mutiny. The fighting came to an end in 1858 and Britain took control of India. In Africa, the British fought several wars for land. The fiercest struggle was against the Boers (Dutch farmers who had settled in Africa). The Boer War lasted from 1899 to 1902. By the end of the war, Britain ruled most of South Africa.

The Victorians built British-style buildings all over the Empire. The Victoria Terminus Railway Station in Mumbai, India, was completed in 1887.

Trading around the world

Countries in the Empire sold their goods to Britain and bought British goods in return. Goods imported from the colonies included tea, spices, cotton, sugar and rubber. Cotton was an especially valuable import for Britain. It was made into cloth and clothing and sold around the world.

Exploring Africa

Some daring explorers led expeditions in Africa. Doctor David Livingstone travelled the length of the Zambezi River in southern Africa. Richard Burton and John Hanning Speke searched for the source of the River Nile in East Africa.

David Livingstone was a Christian missionary, a doctor and an explorer. On his journey along the Zambezi River he discovered an enormous set of waterfalls, which he named the Victoria Falls.

Rich and poor

Social class was very important in Victorian society. People who belonged to the upper and middle classes enjoyed a comfortable way of life. But members of the working class had to work incredibly hard. If they lost their jobs, they faced the terrible fate of being sent to the workhouse.

Rich Victorian girls wore loose dresses. Boys usually wore jackets and knickerbockers.

Life for the rich

Wealthy Victorians lived in large houses and had servants to look after them. The servants cooked and served their meals and even helped them to get dressed. Young children were cared for by nursery maids. Children spent a lot of time in their nursery, which was a large room filled with books and toys.

Life for the poor

Poor families lived in very crowded homes. It was not unusual for a whole family to share a single room. Often, both parents went out to work, and the older children were left in charge at home. Some children helped their parents at work or had jobs of their own.

Poor children played games in the street. These young chimney-sweeps are dancing to the music of a street organ.

Life in the workhouse

Families with no money were sent to the local workhouse. Workhouses were large, bare buildings divided into sections for men, women and children. People in the workhouse had to work long hours at pointless jobs, such as breaking up stones, and they never had enough to eat.

This Lancashire workhouse was completed in 1868. It was much more comfortable than many workhouses, but it was still a grim and frightening place.

Working life

W ork in Victorian times depended on social class. Many upper-class men did not need to work because they had inherited money, houses and land. Middle-class men had well-paid jobs as doctors, lawyers, vicars or army officers. Men and women with a little education could work as teachers or shop assistants, but they were not well paid.

Victorian factories were dark, noisy and dirty.

Factory workers

Thousands of people worked in Britain's factories. The work was very tiring and badly paid and people often suffered accidents. In the early years of Victoria's reign, children as young as six were employed in factories. By the 1830s, however, reformers like Lord Shaftesbury were campaigning for change. Between 1833 and 1901 the British government passed a series of Factory Acts. These acts reduced working hours and made it illegal to employ any children under nine years old.

In this picture of a cloth-weaving factory, you can see a child crawling under a loom to remove some rubbish. Many children were injured at work and some were even killed by moving machinery.

Miners

In the early Victorian period, men, women and children worked in coal mines. Small children crouched by trap doors, holding them open for carts carrying coal. Larger boys dragged heavy carts. In 1842, the Mines Act made it illegal for women and children under ten to work underground in mines, but men and older boys still risked their lives to dig up coal.

Servants

Many working-class people worked as servants. Women took jobs as maids or cooks. Men worked as grooms or gardeners. Some servants had very responsible jobs. The butler and the housekeeper ran the household, working closely with the master and mistress of the house.

Young children often worked as servants. They had a hard and tiring life.

Health and medicine

Victorian towns and cities were very unhealthy places, especially in the first half of the 19th century. Factory chimneys belched out smoke, drains and sewers often overflowed, and rivers were stinking and polluted.

In this Victorian cartoon, the figure of Death is rowing down the filthy River Thames in London.

Dirty towns

Poor families lived in crowded slums, and sometimes up to 30 people shared a single toilet. In these unhealthy conditions, disease spread fast, and thousands of people died each year from infectious diseases such as influenza, cholera and typhoid.

Some reformers were determined to clean up the towns, and many improvements were made in the late 19th century. New sewage pipes were laid, streets were cleaned, and rubbish was collected. Gradually, the rivers became less polluted and the water in cities became safer to drink.

Unhealthy hospitals

In the early years of Queen Victoria's reign, hospitals were dirty and frightening places. Doctors did not wash their hands after treating patients. Surgeons did not clean their instruments and there were no anaesthetics to put patients to sleep. Many people died soon after an operation, and infection spread rapidly through hospital wards.

Victorian city streets were often filled with a thick, black mist, known as smog. Smog was caused by a mixture of winter fog and the filthy smoke from chimneys and trains.

Better care

Hospital care improved greatly during Victoria's reign. In 1847, chloroform gas, a form of anaesthetic, began to be used for operations. Then, in 1869, Joseph Lister invented an antiseptic spray to kill germs. The use of antiseptics led to a dramatic drop in hospital deaths. Nursing care became much better too. The famous nurse, Florence Nightingale, insisted that nurses should be properly trained. She also campaigned for better hygiene in hospital wards.

Florence Nightingale was an army nurse in the Crimean War. Later, she worked in British hospitals. She was known as 'the lady of the lamp' because she went round the wards at night, carrying a lamp.

A schoolchild's day

By the 1870s all children in England had to go to school. This fictional diary entry describes a typical day in the life of a ten-year-old schoolboy.

My day starts badly when I am two minutes late for school. Mr. Banks, my teacher, says I must be punished. He makes me put out both my hands and hits them with a cane. It hurts a lot!

Our first lesson is writing. We copy down sentences onto our slates. Mr. Banks says I am so good at writing I can start using a pen and copy book!

The next lessons are reading and arithmetic. In arithmetic, we recite the twelve times table.

We also have to do some multiplication sums. I make three mistakes and Mr. Banks is very cross. He sends me to sit in the corner with a dunce's cap on my head.

At lunchtime, I eat the baked potato I brought from home, and I play in the schoolyard with my friends. It is the best part of the day!

In the afternoon, we have geography. We have to learn the capital cities of all the countries in the British Empire. Last of all, we have drill. We march round the yard in circles and touch our toes twenty times.

School ends as usual at 5pm. Then I have to walk the three miles home. I have lots of books to carry so I can study for a test tomorrow. Being a schoolchild is very tiring!

The diary entry on this page has been written for this book. Can you create your own diary entry for a Victorian child who works in a factory or who is a servant in a grand house? Use the facts in this book and in other sources to help you write about a day in their life.

Scientists and inventors

Some Victorian scientists made exciting discoveries. Their experiments with electricity led to the invention of the electric light and the telephone. Queen Victoria's reign was also a time of new ideas. Charles Darwin's theory of evolution changed the way that many people saw the world.

Electric light

In the 1830s, the English scientist Michael Faraday discovered a way to produce electricity. This discovery led to the invention of the light bulb. In Britain, Joseph Swan invented his light bulb in 1878. Two years later in the USA, Thomas Edison produced his design. By the 1890s, electric lamps were starting to appear on the streets, but most homes were still lit by gas lamps.

Swan's light bulbs contained a fine carbon filament (thread) which lit up when an electric current was passed through it. His bulbs were used all over Victorian Britain.

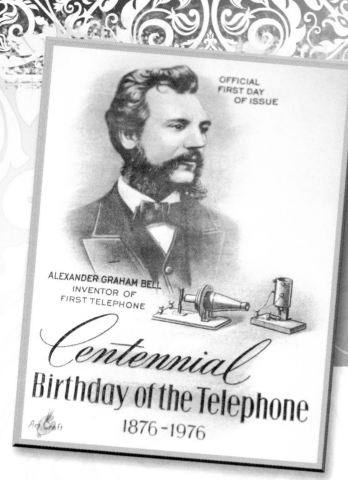

OFFICIAL
FIRST DAY
OF ISSUE

ALEXANDER GRAHAM BELL
INVENTOR OF
FIRST TELEPHONE

Centennial
Birthday of the Telephone
1876–1976

Telegraphs and telephones

The electric telegraph was invented in Britain in 1837. It worked by sending electrical signals down a wire cable. Almost 40 years later, Alexander Graham Bell, a Scotsman living in the USA, discovered how to send voice signals down a cable. In 1876, he demonstrated the first telephone.

This poster celebrates the invention of the telephone. It shows Alexander Graham Bell with his telephone speaker and receiver.

Darwin's big idea

Charles Darwin devoted his life to studying the natural world. In 1859, he published a very important book called *On the Origins of the Species*. The book explained Darwin's theory of evolution. It stated that all life on Earth had evolved (developed very slowly) over millions of years. A lot of people were upset by Darwin's theory because they believed that God had created the world in seven days.

Charles Darwin is shown as an ape in this cartoon. Many Victorians hated the idea that humans had evolved from apes.

19

Engineers and builders

The Victorian age was an exciting time for engineers and builders. Engineers designed railway tracks, canals, tunnels and bridges, as well as many different forms of transport. Architects and builders tried out different styles and building materials.

The Clifton Suspension Bridge, in Bristol, was one of Brunel's first projects. He used strong steel cables to support the weight of his bridge.

Isambard Kingdom Brunel
The greatest engineer of the Victorian age was Isambard Kingdom Brunel. He created the Great Western Railway, which ran from London to Bristol and covered a total of 440 kilometres (273 miles). This enormous project involved designing the engines and the railway tracks, and planning all the bridges, tunnels and stations.

Tower Bridge in London was opened in 1894. It was built in the gothic style, with twin turrets that look like castles.

Victorian buildings

Victorian architects liked to copy styles from the past. They designed many buildings in the gothic style, which was copied from the castles and churches of the Middle Ages. Builders constructed houses, schools and churches all over Britain and the Empire. They also worked on some very large buildings, such as museums and railway stations.

Glass and iron

The Victorians used glass and iron to build enormous structures that were filled with light. The biggest building made from glass and iron was the Crystal Palace. It was built to contain the Great Exhibition of 1851, which was organised by Prince Albert. One of the aims of the Great Exhibition was to show off British engineering skill, and the Crystal Palace was the most impressive exhibit of all.

The Crystal Palace had to be tall enough to fit some trees that were growing in Hyde Park. At its highest point it measured 39 metres (128 feet).

All kinds of transport

At the start of the 19th century, people made journeys on foot, on horseback, or in horse-drawn carriages. If they crossed the sea, they went on ships that were powered by sails or oars. By the end of Victoria's reign, many new forms of transport had been invented. People could travel by train, tram or motorbus. They could ride a bicycle or drive a car, and even cross the ocean in a steam-powered ship.

HMS Warrior was built in 1860. It was driven by steam and was mainly made of iron. The early steamships had sails as well as steam engines.

Travel by rail

Trains began to take passengers in the 1820s, and, by the 1840s, travel by rail had become very popular. Soon, Britain was covered by a network of railways linking the major towns. The world's first underground train opened in London in 1863. It was powered by steam, but later underground trains had electric motors.

Changing bicycles

The first pedal bicycles date from the 1840s. By the 1860s people were riding cycles called velocipedes. They had wooden wheels with iron rims and were so uncomfortable to ride that they were nicknamed 'boneshakers'. Over the next 20 years there were several changes in bicycle design, until the safety bicycle was invented in the late 1880s. The safety bicycle was similar in shape to a modern cycle but it had solid rubber tyres.

In the early 1880s, designers tried out different shapes for bicycles. Some bicycles had wheels of different sizes and were very hard to ride!

Cars, motorbuses and trams

Motor cars were first produced in Germany in the 1880s, and they soon appeared on British roads. In the 1890s, motorbuses started to replace the old horse-drawn carriages. At the same time, electric trams were introduced in some cities.

A Victorian tram in action at the Beamish Museum, in North-East England. Trams ran along rails set into the road. They were powered by electricity which was delivered through overhead cables.

23

Writers, artists and photographers

T he Victorian period was a great time for writers, artists and photographers. Books and magazines were produced cheaply on steam-driven printing presses. People visited art galleries, and the new art of photography took off.

Lewis Carroll's story of *Alice's Adventures in Wonderland* was illustrated by Sir John Tenniel. It was followed by *Through the Looking Glass*, which also had pictures by Tenniel.

Telling stories

Some outstanding writers worked in Victorian times. Charles Dickens wrote page-turning novels, such as *David Copperfield* and *Oliver Twist*. His stories were often written as serials for magazines, with a new part appearing every few months. In 1847, two remarkable sisters published best-selling novels. Charlotte Brontë wrote *Jane Eyre* and Emily Brontë was the author of *Wuthering Heights*.

During Victoria's reign, books written for children became very popular. Lewis Carroll's stories of Alice were an instant success. Other best-selling children's books were *Treasure Island* by Robert Louis Stevenson and *The Jungle Book* by Rudyard Kipling.

Painting scenes

The Victorians loved pictures that told a story. Some artists painted sad pictures, showing sick children. Others produced romantic scenes of mountains and lakes. One group of artists, called the Pre-Raphaelites, was inspired by the Middle Ages. They painted scenes of knights and ladies.

These Victorian paintings are displayed in the Victoria and Albert Museum in London. The Victorians liked to hang their pictures close together.

Taking photographs

Cameras had been used since the 1820s, but they were very hard to operate. Then, in the 1840s, William Henry Fox Talbot invented a simpler way of taking photographs. He used a box camera that contained a special kind of photographic paper. Soon, many people were working as photographers and had set up studios to take portraits.

Some Victorian photographers produced very artistic pictures. This portrait is by the famous artist-photographer Julia Margaret Cameron.

Make a thaumatrope

The Victorians were fascinated by optical illusions. Children played with a toy called a thaumatrope, which produced an illusion when it was spun very fast. You can follow these simple instructions to make your own thaumatrope.

You will need:

Thick card

Paper

Scissors

Pencil, crayons or felt-tip pens

Two long elastic bands

1 Cut out a circular disc from a piece of thick card. The disc should measure about 10cm across. Lay your disc on a large piece of paper and draw around it twice to create two circles.

2 Draw a picture on each of your paper circles. The Victorians often showed a bird and an empty cage. Make sure your bird is small enough to fit inside the cage. Cut out your paper circles and stick them to each side of your disc. The cage should be upside-down.

3 Make a hole on either side of the disc. Then thread an elastic band through each hole. Pull both bands tight so they are firmly fixed to the sides of the disc.

4 Loop the ends of the two elastic bands around your thumbs. Then ask a friend to twist your disc round and round, until the elastic bands feel really tight round your thumbs.

5 Now let the thaumatrope spin. You will experience an optical illusion as the two pictures combine.

How does it work?

The thaumatrope produces an optical illusion because your brain cannot keep up with its changing images. Your brain first sees the picture of the empty cage. Then it sees the second picture of the bird. But it has not finished the process of seeing the picture of the cage, so you see two images at once. This effect is called 'persistence of vision'.

Facts and figures

The Great Exhibition was held in the Crystal Palace in Hyde Park, London, from May to October 1851. It was an amazing success.

• The Crystal Palace covered an area the size of four football pitches.

• Over 13,000 exhibits were on display.

• The biggest exhibit was a hydraulic lifting engine. It was operated by just one man but could lift a weight of a thousand tons.

• Over six million visitors came to see the Great Exhibition.

• Queen Victoria and her family made a total of 13 visits.

Victorian inventions:

Bicycles
Telephones
Postage stamps
Lawn mowers
Chocolate bars
Safety matches
Christmas cards
Christmas crackers
Package holidays
Light bulbs
Underground trains
Vacuum cleaners
Rubber tyres
Public flushing toilets
Chocolate Easter eggs

During Queen Victoria's reign:

• The population of Great Britain doubled from 16 million to 37 million people. (Today it is over 63 million.)

• The average life expectancy in Britain rose from 39 to 48. (Today it is 79.)

• One quarter of the world's total population lived in the British Empire.

All figures used on these pages are approximate.

Glossary

anaesthetic A drug or gas given to patients before an operation to stop them feeling pain.

campaign To work to change or achieve something.

cholera A very serious disease that causes severe sickness and diarrhoea.

colony A place that has been settled in by people from another country and is controlled by that country.

drill A kind of physical exercise with strict rules.

dunce's cap A hat that someone has to wear to show that they are stupid.

empire A group of countries that are governed and controlled by another nation.

evolution The gradual development of living things over millions of years.

export To send goods to another country to be sold.

fictional Made up or invented.

gothic A style of architecture that is copied from the churches and castles of the Middle Ages.

governess A teacher who instructs pupils in their own home.

groom Someone who looks after horses.

hygiene Cleanliness and freedom from germs.

illegal Against the law.

import To bring foreign goods into a country.

industrial To do with factories and making things.

influenza An illness that gives you a high temperature and makes you feel weak. Influenza is often known as flu.

inherit To receive money or land from someone who has died.

knickerbockers Baggy trousers that end just below the knee.

optical illusion Something that you think you see, but which is not really there.

polluted Poisoned by waste and rubbish.

printing press A large machine for printing books, newspapers and magazines.

recite To say something aloud that you have learnt by heart.

sewers Pipes that carry waste.

slums Overcrowded homes where very poor people live.

telegraph A message sent through wire cables.

thaumatrope A Victorian toy made from a circle of card that is spun very fast to produce an optical illusion.

typhoid A very serious disease that causes fever and diarrhoea.

Further reading

Tracking Down: The Victorians in Britain, Liz Gogerly (Watts, 2013)
Men, Women and Children: In Victorian Times, Peter Hepplewhite (Wayland, 2012)
Children in History: Victorians, Kate Jackson Bedford (Watts, 2011)
The Gruesome Truth About: The Victorians, Jillian Powell (Wayland, 2012)
Craft Box: The Victorians, Jillian Powell (Wayland, 2013)
History Snapshots: The Victorians, Sarah Ridley (Watts, 2011)

Websites

http://www.bbc.co.uk/schools/primaryhistory/victorian_britain/
A BBC website designed for children, including sections on children's lives and an interactive time-capsule game.

http://www.show.me.uk/topicpage/parents/pVictorians.html
A collection of museum sites on the Victorians, including games, puzzles, and video tours.

http://www.bbc.co.uk/history/british/victorians/
A BBC website written by subject experts, including sections on the Industrial Revolution, technology and innovation, and daily life.

http://www.bl.uk/learning/histcitizen/victorians/victorianhome.html
A British Library website written by subject experts, including sections on transport, crime, health and the Great Exhibition.

Index

Explore!

Who were the Victorians?
Queen Victoria's reign
Empire and exploration
Rich and poor
Working life
Health and medicine
A Victorian schoolchild's diary
Scientists and inventors
Engineers and builders
All kinds of transport
Artists, writers and photographers
Make a thaumatrope
Facts and figures

978 0 7502 8037 2

Who were the Romans?
The rise of Rome
A mighty power
The Roman world
Town and country
Family and school
Religion and worship
A Roman child's day
Entertainment and leisure
Building technology
Artists and writers
Make a mosaic
Facts and figures

978 0 7502 8098 3

What was World War One?
The war begins
A terrible struggle
A worldwide war
A soldier's day
New technology
Send a message in Morse code
Planes, airships and submarines
Women at war
On the home front
Picturing the war
After the war
Facts and figures

978 0 7502 8027 3

Who were the Ancient Egyptians?
Early kingdoms
A mighty power
The Egyptian world
Religion and beliefs
Everyday life
A day at a temple school
Feasting and fun
Brilliant buildings
Medicine, science and magic
Art, music and writing
Write in hieroglyphics
Facts and figures

978 0 7502 8097 6

What was World War Two?
The war begins
A worldwide war
The final stages
The holocaust
On the home front
Keeping safe
A letter from wartime London
Science in war
Send a coded message
Technology in war
Picturing the war
Facts and figures

978 0 7502 8038 9

Who were the Ancient Greeks?
Early Greeks
A great civilization
The Greek world
Family life
Gods and goddesses
Games and plays
A day at the Olympic Games
Make a theatrical mask
Maths, science and medicine
Architects and builders
Art and ideas
Facts and figures

978 0 7502 8099 0

Who were the Tudors?
Two powerful kings
Edward, Mary, Elizabeth
Rich and poor
A kitchen-maid's day
Making Tudor gingerbread
Tudor towns
Tudor entertainments
Exploring the world
Traders and settlers
Science and technology
Artists, musicians and writers
Facts and figures

978 0 7502 8036 5

Who was William Shakespeare?
Young William
A great success
All sorts of plays
Shakespeare's England
The wider world
Shakespeare's London
The Globe Theatre
Make a model theatre
Actors and playwrights
A boy actor's day
Music and art
Facts and figures

978 0 7502 8135 5